D1249780

Books to grow with

WALT DISNEY ® VOLUME 19

A GUIDE TO
FUN AND LEARNING

WALT DISNEY FUN-TO-LEARN LIBRARY

A Guide to Fun and Learning. All rights reserved. Copyright © MCMLXXXIII The Walt Disney Company
This book may not be reproduced, in whole or in part, by mimeograph or any other means.
ISBN 1-885222-10-6
Advance Publishers Inc., P.O. Box 2607, Winter Park, FL. 32790
Printed in the United States of America
0987654321

Walt Disney
Fun-to-Learn Library

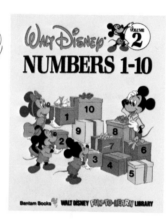

Walt Disney VOLUME 2
NUMBERS 1-10

Walt Disney VOLUME 3
ADVENTURES IN COLORS AND SHAPES

Walt Disney VOLUME 1
ALPHABET A-Z

Bantam Books **WALT DISNEY FUN-TO-LEARN LIBRARY**

Walt Disney VOLUME 4
BIG AND LITTLE, SAME AND DIFFERENT

Walt Disney VOLUME 5
ANIMALS AND THEIR BABIES

Bantam Books **WALT DISNEY FUN-TO-LEARN LIBRARY**

Walt Disney VOLUME 6
REAL-LIFE MONSTERS

Bantam Books **FUN-TO-LEARN LIBRARY**

Walt Disney VOLUME 7
BIRDS AND TREES, FLOWERS AND BEES

Bantam Books **WALT DISNEY FUN-TO-LEARN LIBRARY**

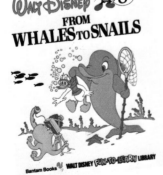

Walt Disney VOLUME 8
FROM WHALES TO SNAILS

Bantam Books **WALT DISNEY FUN-TO-LEARN LIBRARY**

Walt Disney VOLUME 9
OUR WONDERFUL EARTH

Bantam Books **WALT DISNEY FUN-TO-LEARN LIBRARY**

Eighteen exciting volumes introduce your child to important basic concepts and skills....

And there is one volume just for you!

A word from the publisher

Dear Parent,

Walt Disney Studios takes great pride in publishing for your children THE WALT DISNEY FUN-TO-LEARN LIBRARY.

This totally new series is a step-by-step learning experience for youngsters from preschool through the early grades. I know that you and your children will thoroughly enjoy each and every volume, which will help pave the way to better reading skills and good study habits.

The contents of each of the eighteen (18) volumes has been carefully selected. Each book will be irresistibly entertaining, fun to look at, and an educational experience. Each book can be read independently - but used together as a series will form a firm foundation for future learning.

As publishers - we can do no less for the readers of tomorrow!

Sincerely,

Janet Haverley

Janet Haverley
Publisher

The Importance of Early Learning

We are all surprised and delighted by how rapidly young children's bodies develop from the time that they are tiny helpless babies to the time that they head proudly off to school. Even more amazing is their mental development during this earliest stage of life. Experts in child development estimate that 50 percent of a person's intellectual growth occurs during the first four years of life and that another 30 percent is achieved by eight years of age.

Educators agree that since the early years set the pace for growth in later life, food for the mind is every bit as important as food for the body. And special care should be taken to provide young children with "brain food" that is "nutritionally" sound as well as appealing to the eye and palate.

How the Walt Disney Fun-to-Learn Library Can Help Your Child

The books in the Walt Disney Fun-to-Learn Library were carefully planned to give your child a great variety of learning experiences. Each book presents a special topic to help develop background information and concepts in the areas of reading and literature, mathematics, physical and natural science, health, social studies, recreation, and the arts. A look at the book titles will show the wide range of facts and ideas available to your child.

Throughout the Walt Disney Fun-to-Learn Library close attention has been paid to the development of perceptual (sensory) skills, organizing skills, language skills, and reasoning skills. These skills are basic to all learning.

Perceptual skills. Young children take in a vast amount of information through their five senses—sight, touch, taste, smell, and hearing. By relating their new sensations to previously formed impressions, they gradually develop an understanding of colors, shapes, sizes, sounds, flavors, aromas, and textures. The richer the sensory experiences, the better the understanding. The better the understanding, the easier it will be to discriminate, for example, alphabet letters, numbers, words, and kinds of animals.

Organizing skills. After children absorb information, they need ways to organize it for easy storage and recall. They must learn to detect likenesses and differences so they can *classify* objects and ideas into handy categories. For example, they learn by experience that apples, pears, carrots, potatoes, bread, and cereals are all food. The next step is to sort these objects into the appropriate subcategories—fruits, vegetables, and grains. This requires reasoning and classification skills.

Children must also learn to *associate* objects and to arrange them in *sequence* or *series.* An example of association is learning the relationship between a mother cat and her baby kitten. Children become familiar with sequences when they learn that the letters of the alphabet have a definite order and that a story moves from the top line to the bottom line of a page. A familiar example of a series is a row of blocks arranged in order from the smallest to the largest.

Language skills. Early language development begins with a child's hearing and imitating speech sounds until the child has gradually learned to say words and phrases that have meaning. The Walt Disney Fun-to-Learn Library pays special attention to helping your child develop a good broad vocabulary. Many

new words are illustrated, and others are explained within the context of interesting stories. Readiness for reading is encouraged by the introduction of the alphabet, along with the sounds of letters. In addition, simple words that children can learn to read by sight throughout the text are repeated frequently.

Reasoning skills. Just as children need to use their senses to gather information and language to express ideas, they also need to relate ideas to each other in order to think logically. Reasoning skills include understanding, for example, that heat from the sun causes an ice cube to melt and that if you are nice to people, they are apt to be nice to you. Many concepts of math, science, and social studies, as well as the ability to figure out a puzzle, a joke, or a riddle, are based on logical reasoning.

Using the Guide

The following pages of *A Guide to Fun and Learning* will familiarize you with all of the 18 children's books in the Walt Disney Fun-to-Learn Library and give you helpful ideas for using the books with your child. The books are discussed in numerical order, and each book has its own two-page spread. First, you will find colorful sample pages showing the Disney characters featured in the book and typical content. This is followed by a brief description of the book and a list of the skills and concepts it teaches.

Next, you will find a section filled with specific ideas for *using* the book. This section will show you how to introduce the book and will suggest different activities and games to play as you reread it in successive sittings. Particular attention is paid to helping your child get maximum educational value from the book.

Children always delight in carrying what they have learned into everyday activities. We have therefore included a selection of Fun-to-Learn Activities for you and your child to use after you have read each book. These activities include games, stories, rhymes and finger plays, and arts and crafts. Each activity has an educational purpose, but its final selection was made because each one has proved to be lots of fun for lots of children just like yours!

Bb

Baloo the bear has a basket of berries in front and a bee in back.

berries

bear

basket

bee

bird

bed

baby

ball

book

bell

boat

Goofy reads a book to the baby in bed, but the baby wants to play with the ball.

Pooh rings the bell on the boat while the bird keeps watch.

Alphabet A–Z (Volume 1) is designed to develop important beginning reading skills. It will help your child

- recognize capital and lowercase letters
- associate letters with their common sounds
- learn the order of letters in the alphabet
- build a sound vocabulary for reading

Using **Alphabet A–Z**

Encourage your child to browse through the book to find favorite Disney characters, enjoy the different situations, and point out familiar objects. Then work through the book more carefully, introducing one letter and its associated sounds at a time. The frequent review pages are designed to reinforce learning by encouraging children to identify sounds for themselves.

Introducing letters. First, point to the large letters at the top of the page and name both the *capital* and *lowercase* letters. (For very young children you may refer to them as *big* and *little* letters.) Then ask your child to trace the letters with a forefinger and repeat the letter names.

Sounds of letters. As you discuss the pictures and read the sentences, you can stress the beginning sound of words that start with the featured letter.

Help your child name the labeled objects and read the labels. At the same time, point out that all the words begin with the same letter and the same sound. Then help your child think of other words and names that begin with the given letter and sound.

Order of letters. Leaf through the volume quickly, reading together the large letters from A to Z. It helps to repeat the alphabet many times throughout the day with your child. You may also enjoy singing the 26 letters together in the Alphabet Song.

Reading words. After your child knows the individual letters, talk about how the letters work together to make words. Using the pictures as clues, help your child find favorite words. Say each letter in turn, moving from left to right. Point to the letters again, and slowly sound out the word. Repeat the word normally.

Help your child find familiar words in the sentences and in other Walt Disney Fun-to-Learn books. *My First Wordbook* (Volume 16) provides many opportunities to learn additional fun words.

Fun-to-Learn Activities

Alphabet Match

Write the capital letters on 26 index cards and the lowercase letters on another 26 cards. Shuffle each deck separately and place the decks facedown, side by side. Players take turns exposing the top card on each deck and naming the letters. If the letters match, the player keeps them and takes another turn. Letters that do not match are discarded. When all the cards have been used, the player with more matching pairs wins the game.

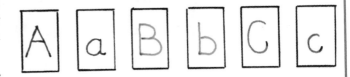

Write It Right

Most children are eager to learn to write letters, names, and words. Use the handwriting models below to show your child the correct way to form each letter. A good way to practice is to "write" with a forefinger or a stick in sand placed in a shallow box. A quick shake of the box will erase any mistakes.

3 three

While Morty and Ferdie are helping Minnie in the kitchen, *three* more guests come racing up Minnie's front walk. It is Huey, Dewey, and Louie.

MINNIE MOUSE

How many presents are Donald's nephews bringing? How many wheels does Louie's tricycle have? How many birds do you see?

In *Numbers 1–10* (Volume 2), Minnie plans a surprise birthday party for Mickey. This delightful story will help your child

3 recognize numbers and numerals *1* through *10*

4 read number words *one* through *ten*

1 learn the order of numbers

2 begin to think about adding and subtracting

Using **Numbers 1–10**

On the first reading, go right through the book with your child and together enjoy Mickey's surprise birthday party. On successive sittings, spend more time talking about the number ideas. For very young children you may want to introduce one number at a time. Use the frequent review and problem-solving pages to reinforce counting skills and to build readiness for addition and subtraction.

Introducing numbers. Start by reading the large *numeral* at the top of the page; then point to the *number word* and read it. Next, read the text and discuss the pictures. Help your child *count* the characters or objects mentioned in the text. Point to each object as you count it and conclude, for example, "There are four packages in all." Help your child count to answer the "How many?" questions. As you finish each little scene, refer back to the large numeral and explain that it tells us the *number* of objects in the group. Say that the number word tells us the same information in another way.

Order of numbers. Each time you count, you start with 1 and name the numbers *in order* until you reach the total number of objects in a group. A good way to help your child learn the order of numbers is to count aloud as often as possible.

You can also leaf quickly through *Numbers 1–10*, reading only the large numerals *1* through *10*. Then repeat, this time reading the large number words *one* through *ten*.

Adding and subtracting. Several problem-solving pages in the book present put-together and take-away situations that form the basis for understanding addition and subtraction. Most young children will arrive at an answer by counting the objects. For older children you may want to introduce the idea of plus and minus.

Fun-to-Learn Activities

Counting Rhymes

Teach your child action rhymes and finger plays such as the following:

THE BEEHIVE

(Form a fist to represent the beehive. Uncurl one finger at a time, starting with the thumb, as the bees are counted.)

Here is the beehive. Where are the bees?
Hiding inside where nobody sees.
Watch and you'll see them come out of the hive
—One! Two! Three! Four! Five!

Writing Numerals

Use the handwriting models below to show your child how to form numerals *1* to *10* correctly. If you cut pictures of one to ten objects from magazines and paste them on pieces of paper, you can have your child count the objects in each group and write the correct numeral nearby.

Number Stories

Your child will enjoy showing off his or her knowledge of numbers as you read favorite stories together. Some examples are "The Three Little Pigs" and "The Brave Little Tailor." Another, "Snow White and the Seven Dwarfs," appears in *Tell Me a Story* (Volume 18 in the Walt Disney Fun-to-Learn Library). Children should also enjoy counting characters and objects in the other Walt Disney Fun-to-Learn Library volumes.

Adventures in Colors and Shapes

blue

The world is full of color, everywhere we look. Is there one color you like best of all?

Cinderella's favorite color is blue. Here she is in her blue dress, dancing with her handsome prince.

"I like blue, too," says the Blue Fairy. "When I wave my wand, I can make everything turn blue!"

Look! Pooh is painting the house blue—and Eeyore, too!

Adventures in Colors and Shapes (Volume 3) features wonderful days in the lives of Disney friends. Their adventures will help your child

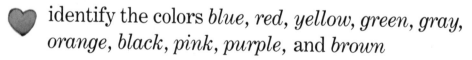 identify the colors *blue, red, yellow, green, gray, orange, black, pink, purple,* and *brown*

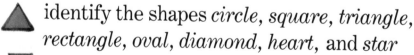 identify the shapes *circle, square, triangle, rectangle, oval, diamond, heart,* and *star*

build a vocabulary of color and shape words

Using **Adventures in Colors and Shapes**

You may want to start by reading clear through this book with your child, or you may prefer to read it in two sittings. The first half of the book introduces colors, and the second half introduces two-dimensional shapes. On successive readings of the book, concentrate on one or two colors or shapes at a time. Use the lively review pages to test your child's understanding and to develop the visual discrimination skills so necessary for beginning readers.

Recognizing colors. To introduce blue, for example, have your child point to all the blue things in the pictures of Cinderella and other friends, repeating the word *blue*. Then ask your child to look around the room and find some blue things — furniture, toys, books and clothing, for example. You may want to explain that there are different shades of blue: light blue, bright blue, dark blue. (For very young children, avoid examples that are close to green.) After your child knows several colors, point out various objects, and have her or him name the color.

Recognizing shapes. The shapes can be introduced in much the same way as the colors. It is especially important with shapes to provide real-life examples for your child to look at and feel.

Always be careful to distinguish between two-dimensional (flat) shapes, such as a circle or square, and three-dimensional shapes, such as a sphere (ball) or cube. Thus, you might say a plate or a hoop has a circle shape, while a ball or an orange is round, or sphere-shaped; in the same way, a floor tile is square, but a building block is shaped like a cube.

In discussing shapes, it is helpful to point out, for example, that a square has four sides of an equal length and four equal corners. A rectangle, on the other hand, has four equal corners and four sides, but two of the sides are longer than the other two.

Fun-to-Learn Activities

Art Projects

Your child will enjoy drawing, coloring, and painting pictures using the colors introduced in the book.

As a *special treat*, make some finger paint in a bowl or cup by stirring several drops of food coloring into some liquid starch. Let your child finger-paint on an enamel top, on a laminated plastic counter, or — oh, joy! — on the refrigerator door. (The paint will clean right off with a wet sponge.) If you want a more permanent record, have your child finger-paint on pieces of wet shelf paper.

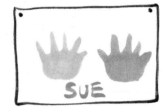

After you have introduced the shapes, you can create a shape game by cutting circles, squares, triangles, and rectangles from colored paper. Your child can arrange these cutouts to make familiar objects and then paste them on a big piece of white or black paper. It is also fun to experiment with various shape and color designs.

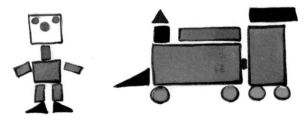

Classification

Children like to sort objects by color or shape or both. For example, when it's time to dress, ask, "What color is your shirt? Can you find some socks to match?" When it's time to pick up the toys, say, "Let's put all the square blocks away first." When you read other books in the Walt Disney Fun-to-Learn Library, ask, "How many green circles can you find on this page? "How many yellow triangles?"

Big and Little, Same and Different

Peter wants to show his friends all of Never Land. He flies *in front of* Wendy to lead the way. Tinker Bell comes along *behind* and watches out for danger.

"Look down there," Peter shouts. "Captain Hook is in trouble." The captain splashes along just in front of the hungry crocodile.

"I'll save you, Captain!" shouts Smee. He is behind the crocodile, and he rows hard to catch up.

In *Big and Little, Same and Different* (Volume 4), Peter Pan and his friends relive their trip to Never Land. On the way, they introduce a wide variety of concepts that your child will need to develop classification and measurement skills. This delightful book will help your child

- tell how objects are the *same* or *different*
- tell the relative size, position, and direction of objects as well as terms relating to the senses
- expand his or her vocabulary

Using **Big and Little, Same and Different**

This book can be read in two ways. At first, your child will probably want you to read straight through it to enjoy the story about Peter Pan and his friends. Later, you can focus more on the concepts presented. In each case, the concept is introduced into the story by a word appearing in italics: for instance, the words *same* and *different* on the first page. The concept is then reviewed on a later page.

Same-different. One of the earliest classification skills young children develop is the ability to point out which of several objects are *different* from the rest and which of the objects are the *same*, or exactly alike. This skill is introduced at the beginning of the book.

Size comparisons. The next set of skills to be introduced are the premeasurement skills. Here your child learns to compare two objects to determine which is *bigger, smaller; longer, shorter; taller, shorter; thicker, thinner.* Then these comparisons are extended to three or more objects. Your child is asked to tell which are the *biggest, smallest; longest, shortest; tallest, shortest.* As you read about each kind of measurement comparison, you can point out some other examples around you.

Directions and positions. This set of skills introduces your child to some very important ideas about locations and movement in space. *Up* and *down* are directional terms. Positional terms include *over* and *under; in front of* and *behind; top, bottom,* and *middle; inside* and *outside;* and *on top* and *under.* As you read these pages with your child, he or she can find other examples of the above concepts within your own surroundings.

Using the senses. The final pages introduce some wonderful words that tell how things feel to the touch: *wet* or *dry; soft* or *hard; smooth* or *rough.* As you read these pages with your child, you both will think of other familiar examples: the texture of a child's clothing, for instance.

Fun-to-Learn Activities

Comparing Sizes

As your child plays with blocks, cars, dolls, and other toys, have her or him identify their sizes. Ask, for example, which of two dolls is *taller,* which of three toy cars is the *longest,* and so on. Or, hold up a particular block and ask your child to sort out all the others that are the *same size,* then all the blocks that are *larger* and *smaller.*

Size Order

As a follow-up to the activity above, challenge your child to line up the toys in *order,* according to their size, length, or height.

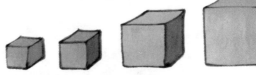

Book of Opposites

To make a book of "opposites," write concepts such as *same-different* and *bigger-smaller* on pieces of paper that have been folded in half, and have your child illustrate them.

The pages can be sewn or stapled together to make a book.

Other Fun-to-Learn Books

All About You (Volume 11) has much more about using the senses. *Ride, Float, and Fly* (Volume 15) will help introduce concepts having to do with movement. Many of the books, including *Animals and Their Babies* (Volume 5), are good sources for size comparisons.

Animals and Their Babies

The baby deer is called a fawn. It can stand and walk almost as soon as it is born. But for a few days the mother may move her fawn from one hiding place to another. She stays nearby, and comes back to feed her baby.

The baby's spotted coat is hard to see in the sun and the shade of the bushes, if the baby stays still. When it is grown, the deer no longer has spots on its coat.

Moose are large animals with huge, spreading antlers. The roar of a bull moose can be heard for miles through the forest.

Shaggy musk-oxen live near the North Pole. When there is danger, they huddle together in a furry circle, with their babies in the middle. Few animals are brave enough to attack the large bull musk-oxen, who stand on the outer ring of the circle. They are afraid of those slashing hooves and sharp horns!

In *Animals and Their Babies* (Volume 5), Mowgli, with the help of the other *Jungle Book* characters, learns about many favorite wild animals and their domesticated relations. This charming book will help your child

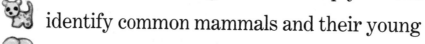 identify common mammals and their young

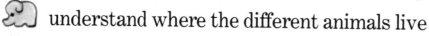 understand where the different animals live

 understand how the animals live from day to day

understand how the animals rear their babies

Using **Animals and Their Babies**

Your child will delight in having you read this book over and over. For the first sittings, let the story carry you along. Later, as your child studies the book in greater detail, focus on one animal family at a time, or on a group of animals that live in one habitat.

Children are eager to learn the names of adult animals and the special names given to their babies. As you read together, you can talk about each animal, what it eats, where it lives, and any other special qualities that distinguish it from other animals in the book.

Your child will especially enjoy learning about the sounds the animals make. What youngster doesn't like to "*Grrrrr*" like a tiger or howl like a wolf?

To a small child one of the most appealing features of mammals is their family life. You might want to talk about the way baby animals mentioned in this book are born and cared for until they can care for themselves.

Fun-to-Learn Activities

Trip to the Zoo

What could be more fun than a trip to the zoo? Plan a special day to let your child see and hear the animals you have read about together in this book. You may want to point out how the zookeepers have tried to make the animals' new homes resemble their natural habitats. Any young animal is, of course, a special thrill for children.

Animal Scrapbook

An animal scrapbook is easily assembled! Help your child cut animal pictures from old magazines and coloring books, sort the animals by family, and paste them into a scrapbook. The names of the animals can be written under the pictures. Encourage your child to draw some favorite animals to add to the scrapbook. You may also want to include photographs of zoo animals or family pets.

Caring for Pets

If you have a dog or a cat, even a young child can help you care for it. Stress that your pet needs fresh food and water each day along with plenty of exercise. A child who does not have a pet at home may be able to learn about a friend's or neighbor's pet.

Animal Homes

Many young children enjoy collecting and playing with small animal models. Shoe boxes make appealing homes for these animals. Help your child paint or "carpet" the bottom and lower sides of the box to represent grass, dirt, and water. You may want to paint a blue sky on the upper sides of the shoe box and paste on a few cotton clouds. Wadded-up paper and other small boxes can be glued or stapled in place to make mountains and caves. Add sand, rocks, and plastic or sculptured-paper trees and bushes to complete the environment. Then introduce the animals to their new homes. When it's time for the animals to go to bed, your child can put the cover on the shoe box and store it away.

Try to imagine an animal as long as six cars put together and as tall as a two-story house! Yet Brontosaurus was harmless to other animals. All it ate was plants. And that long neck must have sometimes been useful to it for reaching its food.

Millions of years ago there lived animals called dinosaurs. The name *dinosaur* means "terrible lizard." Many dinosaurs looked like giant lizards. And they must have looked and sounded "terrible" to the smaller animals that lived many years ago.

"Gawrsh! Look at the size of that bone!" said Goofy, looking at a really large one in the museum.
"That's a Brontosaurus bone," said Mickey. "Brontosaurus was one of the biggest animals that ever lived."

Why are young children so fascinated by dinosaurs? Is it because these strange animals seem scary but are so remote as to be nonthreatening? Whatever the reason, *Real-Life Monsters* (Volume 6) will bring your child many safe and satisfying chills and thrills. It abounds with pre-historic animals and their modern-day counterparts. And it will help your child learn the difference between imaginary dragons and the real reptiles and amphibians of today and long ago.

Using **Real-Life Monsters**

Read through *Real-Life Monsters* with your child at his or her own pace. Take time to stop and talk about the strange and wonderful creatures that particularly take your child's eye. Say their names and help your child wrap his or her tongue around exotic words such as *Brontosaurus* and *Komodo dragon*.

As you reread the book, help your child to sort out which of the animals depicted are, or were, real and which are make-believe. Point out that the animals in this book don't have hair or fur like the animals in *Animals and Their Babies* (Volume 5). Some have scales while others have smooth or horny coverings. Discuss which live in the water, and which live on both water and land. You might also like to emphasize that the baby animals in this book are mostly hatched from eggs, and can usually take care of themselves from the time they are born.

Fun-to-Learn Activities

Field Trips

A rewarding experience for your youngster after reading *Real-Life Monsters* will be a trip to a natural history museum. There he or she can actually see the monstrous size of the prehistoric dinosaurs. Your child may also be able to see dioramas depicting how Earth looked during prehistoric periods.

A trip to the zoo will give your child a chance to see many of the present-day reptiles and amphibians depicted in the book.

Another fun trip is a spring visit to a small farm or woodland pond to see the tadpoles. You may wish to collect a few tadpoles and care for them during their transformation to young frogs. Once they are grown, they can be returned to their natural habitat to help your child learn to respect all living things.

Animal Crafts

Help your child construct snakes, turtles, alligators, and dinosaurs from clay, modeling paste, and other materials. You can use purchased play dough, or you can make your own by employing the following recipe:

HARDENING PLAY DOUGH

1 cup flour
1/3 cup salt
1/3 to 1/2 cup water

Mix the dry ingredients. Stir in the water a little at a time, using only enough to make a dough of modeling consistency.

This kind of dough hardens more satisfactorily when objects molded from it are allowed to air-dry. Coloring can be added to the clay, or the animal models can be painted after they are dried.

Young children love to roll out snakes. Help them prick eyes in the snake with a small pointed stick.

Older children will enjoy rolling, pinching, and patting the clay into more complicated animals. Various other materials can be added to delineate special features. For example, a walnut shell makes a convincing back for a turtle and a length of rickrack trim suggests the pointed scales on a dragon's or a dinosaur's back.

Birds and Trees, Flowers and Bees

"What is making that wonderful smell?" asked Happy.
"Those are wild roses," said Snow White.
"*Yeowtch!*" yelled Grumpy. "They bit me!"
"Oh, Grumpy, roses don't bite," said Snow White. "But they do have thorns. You must be careful when you pick them."

"Snow White, look what I've found!" called Sneezy.
"It's a seedpod full of poppy seeds," Snow White answered. Sneezy turned the seedpod upside down, and out poured its tiny black seeds. "*Aa-CHOO!*" he sneezed.

"Well done, Sneezy," said Doc. "Now that you have spread the poppy seeds on the ground, next spring the bees might have poppy flowers to visit along with this sweet clover."

Children are natural explorers of nature. In *Birds and Trees, Flowers and Bees* (Volume 7) Snow White and the Seven Dwarfs lead the young reader on a remarkable nature discovery tour. This book will help your child

- identify common birds and insects and explore their ways of living
- identify some common plants and trees
- learn about the interdependence of plants and animals

Using **Birds and Trees, Flowers and Bees**

Read *Birds and Trees, Flowers and Bees* many times over with your child, relating the story of Snow White's nature walk to his or her own experiences. For example, have your child point out and name the many familiar birds in the book, and discuss the ones you can see in your neighborhood. As you read about the honeybee, recall when you had honey on toast. (If your child has not tasted honey, now is a good time to plan a special treat!)

As you read about fruits and vegetables, discuss which ones you'd like to have for lunch or dinner. Decide together which trees grow in your neighborhood and which of the flowers grow in the park.

Fun-to-Learn Activities

Nature Walk

Whether you live in the country or city, your child will enjoy a nature walk. Set out to see how many different kinds of plants and animals you can find along the way. Teach your child to stand or sit very quietly to watch the activities of birds and insects. If you leave the plants intact, you can visit them again and again to watch their progress from early spring to late fall. Winter is a good time to talk about trees that stay green year-round. Point out, too, which plants and bushes have seeds and berries for birds to feed on.

Gardening Projects

Help your child plan and plant a garden of his or her own. It may be in a small outdoor plot, in a window box, or in flowerpots on a windowsill. Choose easy-to-grow flowers and vegetables. Marigolds, ageratums, and zinnias are colorful flowers that are simple to grow. Radish and leaf lettuce seeds produce edible vegetables in a short time; beans and corn sprout quickly.

For a windowsill garden, you may want to grow a carrot plant by slicing off the tops of carrots and placing them in a shallow dish of water. You will find easy-to-follow instructions in *Simple Science* (Volume 10). Avocado seeds

and sweet potato vines will also make lovely houseplants.

Impress on your child that plants do need care and will wither and die if they do not get enough water. Like humans, they also need food, which they get from good soil, compost, or occasional fertilizing. Your child will be proud of the beautiful flowers and fresh vegetables he or she has helped to grow. (Again, *Simple Science* has suggestions on caring for a garden.)

Bird Watch

A birdhouse fastened to an easily visible tree or a post makes for a fascinating hobby. Your child will enjoy watching the birds moving in, having babies, caring for their babies, and so on. The bird species that chooses your birdhouse may very well be one illustrated in *Birds and Trees, Flowers and Bees*.

During the winter months you may want to install a bird feeder so that it can be seen from your kitchen or living room window. Ask your child to help you put feed out for the birds at regular intervals, more frequently in very cold weather or snow. Use the book to identify some of the birds you see.

If you cannot have a birdhouse or a bird feeder where you live, perhaps you can arrange to take your child to a big birdhouse at the zoo. It's fun to watch birds from far away in their habitats.

From Whales to Snails

A baby whale is born tail first, instead of head first like many baby animals. It gets a chance to wiggle its body and get its muscles working before its head slips out of its mother's body.

Usually the other whales in the family are circling around to help the mother. One of them may quickly push the baby up to the surface to take its first breath of air.

The baby whale swims close to its mother's side. It plays with the other little whales and practices diving and leaping.

Every child who is fascinated by underwater life will love *From Whales to Snails* (Volume 8). This book introduces plants and animals of the deep as well as those of the seashore and freshwater ponds.

It will help your child

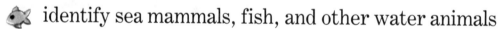 identify sea mammals, fish, and other water animals

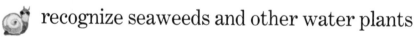 recognize seaweeds and other water plants

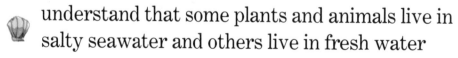 understand that some plants and animals live in salty seawater and others live in fresh water

Using From Whales to Snails

Most young children will be eager to read clear through *From Whales to Snails* to see what is coming next. As you read the book again and again, you may want to spend more time discussing the various families of animals and their habitats.

Sea mammals. Make sure your child understands that the whales, dolphins, and porpoises featured at the beginning of the book are not fish. Along with polar bears, seals, and walrus, they are mammals. They bear live babies, which are fed milk by their mothers. Mammals have bony skeletons and have skin that is usually covered with hair or fur.

Fish. Sharks and the other fish introduced in this book can breathe underwater; they get oxygen through gills in the sides of their bodies. They have bony skeletons, too, but most fish are covered with scales instead of skin. Fins, instead of arms and legs, help them swim. (Your child will find a simple explanation for the special properties of fish when the little Ducks visit Uncle Scrooge's aquarium.)

Mollusks. The octopus, squid, snail, clam, and related animals are mollusks. They have no bony skeletons, but have soft "squishy" bodies. Most mollusks have hard shells to protect their soft bodies.

Crustaceans. Crabs, lobsters, and crayfish belong to another family of animals known as crustaceans. They have "crusty" skeletons on the outside of their bodies. Crabs, lobsters, and crayfish also have pincers instead of hands and a lot more legs than we do!

Fun-to-Learn Activities

Field Trips

What is more fun for young children than a trip to a lakeside beach or the seashore? They adore picking up shells and exploring rock pools. Use such a trip to encourage your child to observe as many water plants and animals as you can find.

If you live near a freshwater pond, plan several excursions at different times of year to observe the plants and animals that make it their home.

A trip to an aquarium or seaquarium is always a special treat. Here your child can see many of the exotic plants and animals featured in *From Whales to Snails*.

Home Aquarium

Caring for your own fish, water plants, and snails can be a very rewarding hobby. You may want to start your child off with a simple goldfish bowl and a goldfish or two. If your child enjoys watching and feeding the fish and retains this interest while helping to clean the bowl, you may want to graduate her or him to a more elaborate aquarium and fancier tropical fish.

Shell Collections

Collecting shells provides a perfect opportunity for you to help your child develop the important classification skills introduced in *Big and Little, Same and Different* (Volume 4). After you have assembled a variety of shells, have your child sort them out in smaller groups. At first, it is easiest to sort the shells according to color or according to shape. Later, encourage your child to sort by both color and shape.

Other Fun-to-Learn Books

Compare the animals in *From Whales to Snails* with those found in Volumes 5, 6, and 7 of the Walt Disney Fun-to-Learn Library. Compare the water plants with the land plants pictured in *Birds and Trees, Flowers and Bees* (Volume 7).

Our Wonderful Earth

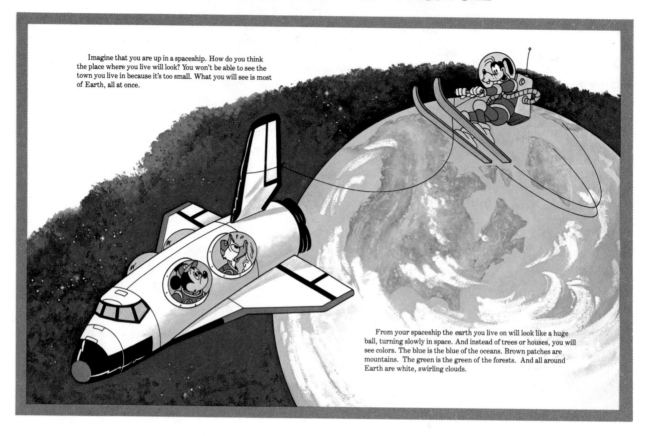

Imagine that you are up in a spaceship. How do you think the place where you live will look? You won't be able to see the town you live in because it's too small. What you will see is most of Earth, all at once.

From your spaceship the earth you live on will look like a huge ball, turning slowly in space. And instead of trees or houses, you will see colors. The blue is the blue of the oceans. Brown patches are mountains. The green is the green of the forests. And all around Earth are white, swirling clouds.

One of children's most precious qualities is curiosity. *Our Wonderful Earth* (Volume 9) will help satisfy your child's curiosity about the wide wonderful world around them and the sky above them. Favorite Disney characters  help your child observe weather patterns and changing seasons and answer questions such as Why is it dark at night? and What does the moon look like up close?

Using Our Wonderful Earth

This is a book to browse through with your child again and again. Enjoy it together at bedtime. Read *Our Wonderful Earth* anew at the beginning of each season. And bring it out again when there is news about exciting new explorations in space.

Carry *Our Wonderful Earth* with you when you go on a trip to help your child identify the physical features of Earth you see—mountains, valleys, rivers, sandy beaches, and so on. Use it, too, to alert your child to changes in climate if you plan to vacation in a different time zone or a different hemisphere.

Fun-to-Learn Activities

Rock Collecting

Encourage your child to collect pebbles and rocks of different kinds. His or her collection may be sorted by color, by how smooth or rough the rocks are, whether they have layers, and so on. Similar rocks should be displayed together to encourage the child's classification skills. Older children who are really hooked on collecting might begin to learn the names of different kinds of rocks and minerals. Such children will especially enjoy a trip to a museum of natural history to see exhibits of rocks, minerals, and gems.

Young rock hounds (and old ones, too) tend to want to save every rock they see! One way to limit the collection is to allot a certain amount of shelf, drawer, or windowsill space to it. As new rocks are discovered, some old ones may be discarded or passed on to friends. You may want to encourage your child to collect only tiny stones or rock bits so that they can be glued into shallow boxes for storage. Or, you may prefer to help your child choose large colorful rocks for display outdoors in a rock garden.

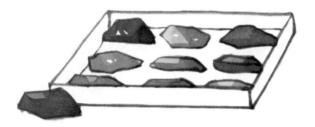

Weather Calendar

A large calendar with a page for each month makes a good weather calendar. Discuss the calendar with your child, explaining how it helps people keep track of the days in a year. Introduce the names of the months and days of the week. Point out, too, that each numbered box on the calendar stands for one particular day. Each evening you can talk about what the weather was like that day—sunny, cloudy, rainy, or snowy. Then help your child draw the appropriate symbol on the calendar.

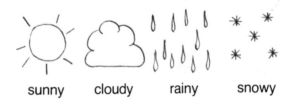

sunny   cloudy   rainy   snowy

Exploring Space

Young children love to stay up late to observe the night sky. Choose a clear night so you can look at the moon and stars together. Talk about how far away they are—the stars much farther than the moon. You might want to explain that the moon travels around Earth while Earth travels around the sun. Later, your child can compare the moon's shape with the phases of the moon pictured in *Our Wonderful Earth*. You might want to point out the North Star, Big Dipper, and other constellations. Ask your child to stand very still and to imagine that he or she feels Earth, and yourselves, moving through space.

If you live near a planetarium, check on programs that may be available for young children. The National Aeronautics and Space Administration or a local museum may also sponsor exhibits on space exploration you can visit together.

Simple Science

A magnet is so strong it will still work when something gets in its way, like a piece of paper

Goofy puts some thumbtacks into the bottom of a cork.

Mickey makes a paper sail with a piece of paper. He uses a pin to put the sail in the cork.

—or like water. Mickey and Goofy are going to make a special sailboat that sails with a magnet. Here's what they need:

paper

thumbtacks

cork

pie plate

pin

shoe boxes

Then he puts a pie plate on two shoe boxes, leaving enough space between the boxes to fit his hand.

Mickey puts the cork boat in the water.

By moving a magnet under the plate, he sails the boat!

In *Simple Science* (Volume 10), the Disney characters explain some very basic science concepts and present experiments you can perform safely and enjoyably with your child. This book will help your child

- understand simple science concepts
- sharpen her or his powers of observation
- learn to experiment, evaluate outcomes, and draw conclusions
- solve problems and think logically

Using **Simple Science**

Simple Science is divided into seven sections. Read and work through one section at a time rather than trying to read the whole book at one sitting. Plan ahead, so you will have the time and materials organized to do the experiments.

Each section in *Simple Science* deals with questions young children frequently ask about objects and happenings around them. Start a section by reading the stories through and telling about what the Disney characters are doing in the pictures. Then you and your child can try out the easy experiments suggested in the text. You may want to explain why you got the results you did at the end of each experiment or activity.

Fun-to-Learn Activities

Seeing Through Things

Roll a piece of paper or light cardboard into a tube about 1 inch in diameter. Tape it in place. Have your child hold the tube to one eye and look at a light or other object. At the same time, have him or her look at a book or hand held in front of the other eye, about halfway along the length of the tube. It will seem to your child that she or he is looking at the light through a hole in the book or hand. This is because each eye is looking at a separate image. Usually we use both eyes together, but when we see images separately, a distortion is created.

Seed Experiments

1. Open different kinds of fruits and help your child find the *seeds*. Discuss the size, shape, color, number, and special features of the seeds. You might explain that some large single fruit seeds, such as those found in peaches, plums, and avocados, are called *pits*. The single seeds in cherries are sometimes referred to as *stones*.

2. Large seeds of various kinds, such as lima beans, corn, pumpkin seeds, and peas, can be soaked overnight. The next day, help your child open the seeds very carefully and look for the tiny plants inside. You may wish to use a magnifying glass to see the plant. Explain that every seed has a baby plant inside and some

food to help the tiny plant grow. (Your child will enjoy trying the growing experiments to be found in *Simple Science*.)

Mirror Experiments

1. Provide a smooth flat mirror and have your child observe his or her own reflection. Have her or him try looking at the inside and then the outside of a shiny metal bowl or spoon. Discuss the difference in the reflections.

2. Show your child how to hold and move a mirror to reflect a spot of sunlight or lamplight on various parts of the wall or ceiling.

Magnifying Glass

Young children love to collect and handle tiny things, such as pebbles, seedpods, and shells. A magnifying glass will help them observe the details of these tiny objects. What can be more fun than the magic of seeing small objects "grow" larger under the glass? Encourage your child to take a magnifying glass out of doors to find tiny insects in the grass or in the cracks of the sidewalk. Help him or her discover the parts of a flower and the flecks of colored minerals in a rock. Indoors, it's fun to see how hairs grow on your arm and to find little air bubbles in a piece of bread.

If binoculars or a spyglass are available, have your child look at distant trees and birds in flight. Looking through the "wrong" end is exciting, too. Now all the big things look little!

All About You

Your bones hold up your body. All your bones together are called your skeleton. You have big bones and small bones inside of you. The biggest are your arm bones and leg bones. The smallest are in your hands and feet. You even have three tiny bones in each ear. Your bones protect the soft inside parts of you, like your heart and lungs.

Your bones are very hard. Because they are hard, they can't bend. But there are places called joints where two bones meet, and luckily, joints can bend. Your elbows, knees, hips, shoulders, wrists, and ankles are all joints.

In *All About You* (Volume 11), Mickey Mouse and his friends investigate what the human body is made of, how it works, and how to take good care of it. This book will help your child

 identify parts of the human body and their functions

 develop awareness of the five senses and how they help us cope with the world

learn good health-care habits

Using **All About You**

Children are always fascinated to learn about their own bodies, so let your child set the pace for using this book. At first you may read quickly through the book, and then later study individual sections in greater detail.

Parts of the body. As you read about various parts of the body and examine the illustrations, point out the parts on your child's own body. Talk about how the parts are used and what they do. The Disney characters featured in the book will encourage your child to develop good health-care habits.

The five senses. As you read together about sight, hearing, smell, taste, and touch, give your child opportunities to think about and use his or her own senses. For example, talk about things that taste sweet, smell good, feel soft, sound loud, and so on. Or let your child cover her or his eyes and try to walk across the room without seeing.

Fun-to-Learn Activities

Body Map

Help your child make a full-scale map of his or her own body. Place a large piece of plain wrapping paper on the floor and have your child lie down on it. Use a marker or crayon to trace around your child's body. Then work together to draw in and label external details such as hair, eyes, nose, mouth, ears, and fingernails.

You may wish to make a second drawing on the other side of the paper to show internal organs, such as the heart, which are depicted in *All About You.*

Growth Records

Help your child keep track of his or her growth. To record changes in height, attach a long vertical strip of paper to the wall and mark it off in inches or centimeters. On birthdays and several times through the year, measure your child, draw a colorful line, and record the date. Your child may want to measure a favorite doll or toy animal on the same strip. At the same time, record her or his weight in a small notebook or

another chart. You may also want to record the dates your child loses teeth, the dates new teeth first peek through, and when they are full grown.

Sensory Surprises

Children love guessing games. This fact can be used to help them sharpen their sensory perceptions. To sharpen the sense of *smell*, for example, let your child help you fill several small opaque jars with nontoxic materials, such as vinegar, peppermint flavoring, cloves, apple slices, and hand lotion. As each material is placed in a jar, identify it and have your child smell it. Mix all the jars, and then have your child uncover one jar at a time, sniff its contents without looking, and guess what is inside. Let him or her look inside to check the answer.

To sharpen the sense of *hearing*, fill small boxes with materials such as sand, pebbles, buttons, marbles, paper clips, and cotton balls. Have your child shake one box at a time and listen carefully, to guess what is inside.

To sharpen the sense of *taste*, place various foods, such as an apple, a slice of lemon, a cookie, a pickle, and a pretzel, on a plate. Blindfold your child. Have her or him taste one food at a time; tell whether it is sweet, sour, salty, or bitter; and guess what it is. Your child can see Donald's nephews playing this taste game in *Simple Science* (Volume 10).

It's a Small World

Rosita and Paco join in the biggest water fight ever. Even mothers and fathers enjoy the fun. It looks as though the children have found the best place to shower their friends with color. Splash! Goofy is blushing red all over! Soon everyone in the town will look like a gaily colored Easter egg.

What are Rosita and Paco doing with all those paper bags full of balloons? They are getting ready for carnival time in Peru. They have brought brightly colored powders to mix with water. Then they will fill each balloon with a different-colored water.

In *It's a Small World* (Volume 12), Mickey Mouse introduces boys and girls from countries all around the world and shows some of their favorite pastimes and festivals. This book will help your child

 understand how people live in various parts of the world

 develop respect for different costumes and customs

think about living, playing, and working together

Using **It's a Small World**

It's a Small World (Volume 12) is a fun book to read over and over. At first, just read it for the stories about children in different countries. On successive readings, focus special attention on one or two countries, and add other information you may have about them.

If you have a world map or globe, you can point out the location of each country and discuss whether it has a hot, cold, or temperate climate. Explain that the climate affects the way people live and the things they do. For example, in Norway children learn to ski, but children in Egypt or Australia can't ski because they have no snow.

As you reread *It's a Small World*, help your child realize that, although there are differences among peoples, there are really more similarities. We all need food, clothing, and shelter. We all need to work and we all love to play. We all have special holidays and festivals that give us an opportunity to celebrate together with our friends and neighbors. In short, it's a small world!

Fun-to-Learn Activities

Dress-ups

Help your child dress up as a boy or girl from another country and dramatize some of the activities in the book. For example, you might provide a sombrero or a gaily embroidered skirt to transform your child into a Mexican child. You could work together to make a piñata from papier-mâché and then have fun breaking it.

Cooking Around the World

If you have a family tradition of special foods, or you like to cook ethnic food, you can use shopping trips or mealtimes to introduce your children to the favorite foods of different nationalities. Your child can help you bake and decorate Scandinavian cookies at Christmastime, for instance, or help choose a favorite form of pasta. Many supermarkets carry foods from foreign lands, such as kiwi fruits, bulgar wheat, oriental noodles, and Mexican tacos.

Field Trip

Museums often have ethnic costumes, masks, and toys from foreign countries. Take your child on a field trip to a local museum, toy museum, or large city museum to see the costumes illustrated in *It's a Small World*, and pick out toys or other interesting objects from countries featured in the book. Children will love, for instance, a nest of dolls from the Soviet Union or a special kite from Japan.

Roots

Even a small child will be fascinated by family stories about the country that parents, grandparents, or great-grandparents came from. Pull out family photographs or other mementos to make the stories more vivid. Or use magazine pictures or postcards to create a special scrapbook of a country or countries for your child.

Other Fun-to-Learn Books

Your child will enjoy reading about more holidays throughout the world in *Seasons and Holidays* (Volume 13). Read *People at Work* (Volume 14) to emphasize that all around this small world, people work to help each other and to earn money to buy food, clothing, and shelter.

Seasons and Holidays

Long ago in England people believed in ghosts, witches, elves, goblins, and all kinds of spooky creatures. So they dressed up in scary costumes to protect themselves. After all, what ghost would harm another ghost?

On Halloween we still dress up in costumes. Why? Because it's so much fun!

Here come Morty, Ferdie, and Donald's nephews now. They want to see if they can scare Daisy.

"I've been waiting for you," says Daisy. "Can you come in to my Halloween party? We'll dunk for apples, eat some pumpkin bread, and then we'll all go trick-or-treating."

Seasons and Holidays (Volume 13) introduces important holidays and seasonal activities. In this book Mickey Mouse and his friends will help your child

 understand holidays and customs associated with them

 identify the four seasons and their related activities

 develop a sense of passing time and order of events

Using Seasons and Holidays

Read through *Seasons and Holidays* several times with your child to familiarize her or him with the seasons of the year and the holidays we celebrate in each one. Talk about the weather in spring, summer, fall, and winter and the seasonal activities your child enjoys as the weather changes. Point out that each old year ends and each new year begins during the winter season.

Seasons. As each season begins, look it up in *Seasons and Holidays* and read about the activities associated with it. Plan together to carry out as many of the activities as you can. For example, fly a kite on a nice windy spring day, make a sand castle in the summer, rake colorful leaves in the fall, and build snow people in the winter.

Holidays. As each holiday approaches, read about it in *Seasons and Holidays*. Discuss the decorations and customs associated with the holiday, and do some of the arts-and-crafts projects suggested in the pictures. For example, cut out paper hearts and glue on lace to make valentines, color eggshells to make Easter eggs, and carve a jack-o'-lantern for Halloween.

Fun-to-Learn Activities

Holiday Calendar

Hang a big calendar where you and your child can mark off the passing days. Discuss the changing seasons, and look ahead to the special holidays noted on the calendar. Help your child learn the days of the week in order and point out how they are shown on the calendar. Also help your child learn the names of the months as they occur. You may want to use the calendar to record special family events or outings that your child can look forward to.

Family Holidays

Some very personal holidays are celebrated by each family — the birthdays of family members. Be sure to record their birthdays on a calendar. Your child can have lots of fun helping to make gifts and plan birthday meals for other members of the family. Of course, the most important birthday of all is the child's own birthday!

The term *holiday* may be used to refer to a family outing or prolonged vacation trip. Discuss when the holiday will occur, how long it will last, where you will be going, and what you plan to do there. Let your child help you prepare for the holiday. And if you take pictures, or collect souvenirs, let him or her help you make a special scrapbook to remember the fun you had.

More Holidays

Your family, friends, and neighbors may celebrate additional holidays, such as the Chinese New Year, Saint Patrick's Day, Memorial Day, Ukrainian Easter, Grandparent's Day, Columbus Day, Arbor Day, or Hanukkah. Explain to your child the background of each new holiday and help him or her share in preparations for it. To celebrate Arbor Day, for example, help your child pick wild flowers or dig up a tree seedling from your garden to take to a grandparent or a shut-in friend.

People at Work

Houses and apartments are built by people called builders. These builders are building a new house for Minnie. First the workers dig a big hole and then they pour in the concrete to make the foundation. Trucks take away all the dirt and bring back the wood the builders will need to make the walls.

People at Work (Volume 14) introduces a wide variety of occupations, explains what workers do, and tells how the everyday things we eat, wear, live in, ride in, and enjoy are made. This book is designed to help your child

- identify workers and learn about their jobs
- develop awareness that people must work to help themselves and each other
- begin to think about future career possibilities
- understand how his or her small jobs at home help the family

Using **People at Work**

Read through *People at Work* several times with your child, pausing to discuss in greater detail workers of special interest to your child. Whenever possible, relate the jobs in the book to jobs held by family members, and by your friends and acquaintances.

As you read *People at Work*, point out that we need different kinds of workers to make things, build things, fix things, take us places, help us when we are in trouble, entertain us, and make our lives better in many ways. Emphasize that everyone who does a job helps everyone else.

You may want to point out that people are usually paid money for their everyday jobs. They then use this money to buy food, shelter, transportation, and other goods and services. Sometimes people do jobs for each other without exchanging money. A good example of this is family members working together to make a happy home life.

Fun-to-Learn Activities

Job Sites

Plan several field trips to acquaint your child with the places where people work. These trips can be as simple as a trip to the grocery store, a local gas station, the post office, or the library. Other trips may take more planning. Perhaps you can team up with a few other parents and children to visit a fire station, a telephone exchange, or dairy. As you and your child walk around the neighborhood, see how many different kinds of workers you can spot. Describe the job each one does and emphasize how that job is important to the people in your community. And if you can, take your children to your own place of work. It is important for children to find out what Mommy and Daddy do when *they* are at work.

Dramatizations

In addition to their own jobs, children will enjoy dramatizing grown-up jobs. Encourage such activities as playing house, directing sidewalk traffic, building (block) houses, nursing a sick teddy bear, and repairing broken objects. These activities will be more fun if your child can dress up in "uniform." Children also love to pack a sandwich, an apple, and a container of milk in a lunch box or brown paper bag to eat later "on the job."

Murals

Attach a long piece of wrapping paper to a wall and help your child make a mural of different kinds of workers. A good way to start is to search through old magazines for pictures of workers, cut them out, and sort them according to where they work and the kinds of jobs they do. The cutouts can be pasted onto the mural paper and painted or colored in. For example, if you have pasted up a doctor and a nurse, you could help your child draw a doctor's office around them or outline a hospital behind them.

Jobs at Home

Plan regular jobs at home for your child. He or she might help you dust the chairs, make cookies, or set the table. And of course, putting toys away is a very special child's job. You can encourage your child to "check off" a job well done on a special roster pinned up in the kitchen.

Other Fun-to-Learn Books

Many people need transportation to get to their jobs, and transportation itself requires people. *Ride, Float, and Fly* (Volume 15) includes some vivid renderings of buses, trains, and airplanes.

Ride, Float, and Fly

"Come along, boys," said Donald. "Ahoy there, all aboard!"
"Aw, Uncle Donald, do we have to?" asked Dewey.
"That old boat doesn't even look as if it will float," said Louie.
"Sure it will," replied Donald, as he led the boys up the gangplank to the deck of the *Daisy D.*
While Donald looked at the charts, maps, and instructions for sailing the *Daisy D.*, the three boys looked at the other boats in the bay.

Louie liked the brightly colored sailboats anchored in the harbor. Each had its own rowboat for bringing passengers to and from the shore. But Huey liked the big, wide fishing boats the best of all. Their huge fishing nets were drying in the sun.

Ride, Float, and Fly (Volume 15) presents three transportation stories. First Minnie and Mickey take a day trip on land. Then Donald takes Huey, Dewey, and Louie for a fabulous boat ride. Finally, Goofy takes his first ride in an airplane. Along the way, your child will learn to

 identify the ways people travel from place to place and transport goods

 classify forms of transportation according to whether they move on land, sea, or air

Using **Ride, Float, and Fly**

Ride, Float, and Fly is a good book to read in sections. The three sections about land, sea, and air transportation are clearly delineated, and each has a story children will enjoy.

Land transportation. As you read the "Ride" section of the book, be sure to point out that all the vehicles described run on land. Most, such as cars, buses, trucks, and roller skates, run on top of the ground. Trains, on the other hand, and sometimes trolleys, run on tracks laid on the ground. Show your child that most forms of land transportation have wheels. (Sleds, of course, have runners.) Land vehicles may use energy from gasoline or diesel oil, electricity, people power, or horsepower.

Water transportation. As you read the "Float" section of the book, point out that nearly all these forms of transportation move from place to place on the water. The submarine can also move under the water. Most ships—with engines—use fuel oil for energy; sailboats use wind power; and canoes, kayaks, and rafts flow with the current or require people power.

Air transportation. As you read the "Fly" section, emphasize that these forms of transportation move from place to place through the air. This section explores the different ways people have devised to become airborne, ending with Goofy watching a spaceship taking off into space.

The last pages, on space travel, will give you a chance to talk about any new space discoveries or technologies. Your child will enjoy comparing the spaceship in *Ride, Float, and Fly* with the spaceships shown in *Our Wonderful Earth* (Volume 9).

Fun-to-Learn Activities

Field Trips

Expose your child to as many kinds of transportation as possible, both as an onlooker and as a rider. As you stroll around the neighborhood, see how many different kinds you can spot. Count both motorized and unmotorized vehicles. More formal field trips might include a visit to the fire station, an automobile showroom, the bus station, the airport, the docks, and a space museum. Use *People at Work* (Volume 14) to talk about the people who work in transportation—from the bus driver to the airline pilot.

Workbench Projects

Scraps of lumber make good cars, boats, and airplanes. You can use precut pieces, or you can encourage your child to saw and hammer for him or herself, under your supervision, of course. Round pieces of wood or bottle caps will make good wheels for a "car" or "train." Children love to paint their finished vehicles with brightly colored water-base paints. Details such as windows and doors may be added with a felt-tip marker.

Traffic Signs

While you are focusing attention on transportation, take the opportunity to acquaint your child with common traffic signs. Be sure your child understands the meaning of each sign. Discuss, also, the meaning of traffic lights. Teach your child that a green light gives cars permission to go, so pedestrians must wait. A red light tells the cars to stop, so after looking both ways, pedestrians can cross the street. When the light is yellow, both drivers and walkers should proceed with great caution.

Flying High

Show your child how to fold a piece of paper to make a paper airplane. Then show her or him how to make it fly through the air.

Your child may also enjoy flying a kite or releasing a helium-filled balloon and watching it sail up in the sky.

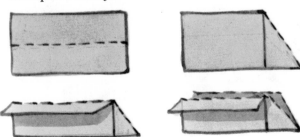

My First Wordbook

On the Farm

"Where can that piglet be?" Grandma Duck wonders. She loves all the animals on her farm, but the baby pig is her favorite.

Crash! The billy goat is in a hurry to get his dinner. Watch out, Donald!

What are the other animals you see in the barnyard?

Labels in illustration: barn, windmill, silo, rooster, sheep, tractor, cow, goat, hat, calf, goose, lamb, pig, hay, hen, piglet, corn, pail, trough, chick

My First Wordbook (Volume 16) is designed to teach young children that everything in their world has a name. Disney friends illustrate a variety of new and familiar words in a broad range of basic categories. The book will help your child

 expand his or her vocabulary

 develop beginning reading skills

 develop classification skills

Using My First Wordbook

My First Wordbook is a book for browsing. Your child will enjoy poring over the pages and demonstrating how many objects he or she can identify. Repeated naming of familiar objects builds confidence and prepares the way for learning new and different words. When you come to a new word, first point to the picture of the object and then read the word itself, explaining that the word tells the name of the object. Have your child repeat the word while pointing to the picture.

On successive sittings, point to one word at a time, moving across the page from left to right and from top to bottom. Ask your child to "read" the word using the pictures as clues. Then, as he or she becomes adept at identifying the words, play a more advanced game. Cover up the picture clue before you point to a word, and ask your child to "guess" what the word is. Afterward, uncover the picture to confirm or correct the guess.

To help your child develop classification skills, talk about how the words in each category go together. You might suggest other words that belong to the same category, using as a source one or more of the other books from the Walt Disney Fun-to-Learn Library. *My First Wordbook*, for example, includes only some of the sea creatures you will find in *From Whales to Snails* (Volume 8).

Fun-to-Learn Activities

Labels, Labels

To emphasize that everything has a name, label your child's belongings and objects around the house.

You may want to write the names in a different color for each category of objects. Thus, words for toys might be blue and words for clothing green.

Learning to Read

Labeling is also effective for teaching beginning reading, as long as you work with only a few words at a time. Pick a category that will interest your child, such as "toys," and label one item the first day. For example, label a doll, making sure your child understands that the word *doll* names the real doll. Trace over the word and spell out the letters.

The second day, review *doll*. After your child reads the word, remove the label and ask him or her to read it in isolation. Then have your child find which toy the label names. Pin the word back on the doll. You are then ready to introduce another word, such as *car.*

If all is going well, you may even introduce a third word. Don't be in a hurry, though. The very idea of written words is pretty sophisticated and is best developed slowly with continued exposure to familiar labels and constant review. Once the idea becomes real to your child, you can progress more rapidly with introducing new words.

Word File

As your child becomes comfortable with the idea of reading words, help him or her make a file of favorite words. Write each chosen word on an index card, and have your child draw a picture to illustrate it.

Have your child sort the word cards into categories and file them in a box.

Other Fun-to-Learn Books

Encourage your child to point out familiar words as you read other books in the Walt Disney Fun-to-Learn Library. Almost all the categories found in *My First Wordbook* can be linked with other books in the series. You might also identify words in the wordbook and then ask your child to see if they can be found on the appropriate pages of *Alphabet A−Z* (Volume 1).

Rhymes and Riddles, Gags and Giggles

Why did Goofy throw butter out the window?

He wanted to see the butterfly.

What time is it when an elephant sits on a fence?

Time to get a new fence.

What do you have when your head is hot, your feet are cold, and you see spots in front of your eyes?

A polka-dot sock on your head.

If the Three Little Pigs were under one little umbrella, why didn't they get wet?

It wasn't raining.

What is more fun than playing with words and exploring the sights and sounds of language? *Rhymes and Riddles, Gags and Giggles* (Volume 17) is designed to help your child

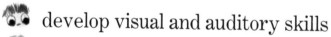 appreciate the rhymes and rhythms of language

 understand that some words have several meanings

develop visual and auditory skills

develop a sense of humor

Using **Rhymes and Riddles, Gags and Giggles**

Rhymes and Riddles, Gags and Giggles is a book your child will want to come back to again and again because it is intended to be used a page or two at a time. It contains a wide selection of puzzle pictures, jokes, riddles, "knock-knocks," word plays, rhymes and rhyming games, funny rebuses, puns, and tongue twisters. Let your child open the book to any section and then begin.

For visual puzzles, read the directions and look at the pictures together, encouraging your child to tell what is wrong with the illustrations. On other pages, read the rhymes, jokes, or riddles, and discuss the pictures. When you come to the tongue twisters, take turns trying to say them, slowly at first and then faster and faster. For the rebuses, you read the words, and let your child name the pictures. Your child will enjoy sharing his or her favorite jokes and riddles with the rest of the family.

Fun-to-Learn Activities

Hide the Penny

Play this game to increase visual and thinking skills. Have your child and other family members go out of the room while you "hide" a penny in plain sight. Let the players come back into the room and walk around to hunt for the penny. They must not touch or move anything. You may give clues by saying, for example, "Benjy is very hot" (meaning nearby) or "Amy is getting cold" (meaning she is moving away from the penny). Each person to spot the penny sits down and the others keep on looking. When all the players have finally found the penny, the first player to do so takes the next turn hiding it.

Picture Puzzles

To help your child develop visual perception, provide picture puzzles for her or him to put together. Start with puzzles with just a few pieces and gradually work up to harder puzzles. You can create your own by pasting magazine or calendar pictures on a cardboard backing and then cutting them into odd-shaped pieces. Some children even have fun putting puzzles together upside down!

Rhyming Plays

Teach your child finger plays, such as the one found on page 9 of *A Guide to Fun and Learning.* Children also love rhyming games, especially those that can be sung or chanted. "The Farmer in the Dell" and "This Old Man, He Played One" are old favorites.

Living Statues

This is a game that always brings peals of laughter from young children. The object of the game is to become the silliest-looking statue ever. In a musical version of the game, the leader plays the piano or a record player while the children wiggle around into different positions and, of course, make funny faces. The leader stops the music and the children "freeze." The leader announces the winner and play continues; this time the winner is the one to signal when the music should stop. He or she then selects the next winner.

In a nonmusical version of the game, the leader calls out, "Twirl." The children twirl around three times (getting dizzy is half the fun!) and then fall into a funny position. The leader chooses a winner, who starts the next game.

Cinderella

Long ago, in a far away kingdom, lived beautiful Cinderella with her stepmother and her two ugly stepsisters, Drizella and Anastasia. She did all the housework for her jealous stepsisters, who made her wear rags and sit in the cinders to keep warm.

But she didn't have a pretty dress to wear. When her stepmother realized that Cinderella wanted to go, she said, smiling wickedly, "First you must wash the windows, scrub all the floors, clean the drapes, and dust the chandeliers. If, when you have finished your work, you have time to make a suitable dress, of course you may go to the ball."

Cinderella knew she would never have enough time to make herself a ball gown. Sadly, she began to do all the chores. But her friends, the mice, had also heard the stepmother's words. Chattering excitedly, they collected ribbons and beads thrown into the garbage by Drizella and Anastasia, and made a beautiful ball gown for Cinderella out of an old dress they found in her cupboard.

As Cinderella ran down the stairs in her new dress, her stepmother and stepsisters were furious to see how lovely she looked. "Those are my beads!" and "That's my ribbon!" they shrieked, as they tore Cinderella's dress to pieces.

In the kingdom, there lived a lonely prince. The king decided to invite all the unmarried girls to a ball so that the prince could choose a wife. The stepsisters were going, and Cinderella wanted to go with them.

Tell Me a Story (Volume 18) contains two kinds of stories. First, there are three Disney favorites—"Cinderella," an incident from "Bambi," and "Snow White and the Seven Dwarfs." Then there are several delightful retellings of old fables with Disney folks as the main characters. This book will help your child

 develop an interest in reading

 enjoy entertaining stories

 learn simple moral concepts

Using **Tell Me a Story**

This book is organized so that you can read one story at a time, or perhaps two. Take time to discuss the pictures as you go and explain any new words or strange ideas. Let your child tell you how he or she feels about the characters and their actions.

Your child will want you to read some of the stories over and over, perhaps even before you have completed the whole book. As you reread the stories, pause occasionally and let your child fill in the details or complete the story. Later, ask your child to retell the whole story. You may use prompting questions, such as "What did she do then?" or "What happened next?" to help her or him get the events in the correct sequence.

Encourage your child to listen to new stories as well as to old favorites. As you read the fables, talk about what happens to the characters and the simple morals illustrated. Wherever you can, relate the morals to your own family situation or your children's experiences with their friends.

Fun-to-Learn Activities

Puppet Show

Your child might enjoy dramatizing favorite stories using hand puppets, or stick puppets. Finger puppets can be made in a few minutes by rolling a cylinder of paper around the child's finger and taping it together. The child can draw and color a simple character to glue on the front of the cylinder to make the puppet.

Work together to retell the story, pretending that the puppets are doing the talking and performing the actions described in the story. This is a good way to teach children how to put actions in the proper sequence.

Dramatizations

Your child may enjoy dressing up as a favorite Disney character and acting out some of the events in one or more of the stories. You may want to arrange a special time for sharing the "play" with other members of the family.

Personal Stories

Most children adore being the main character in a story you tell at bedtime. A favorite is a true story about "When you were a little baby." Other true stories might recount what happened when your child went to the hospital, visited Grandmother, or had a birthday party. Fantasy stories are also fun. Try making up stories in which your child flies to the moon, meets a fairy godmother, rescues a missing kitten, or drives a giant bulldozer. Be sure to have a happy ending, and don't be surprised when you are asked to repeat the story many times.

Encourage your child to make up stories about him or herself. Provide art supplies so that she or he can illustrate the stories. Crayon drawings on typewriter paper are easily stapled together to make a booklet. Or, your child might prefer to draw or paint the actions on a large piece of shelf paper and display them on a clothesline.

Other Fun-to-Learn Books

Many of the other books in the Walt Disney Fun-to-Learn program contain entertaining stories. For example, *Big and Little, Same and Different* (Volume 4) recounts the adventures of Peter Pan. *Ride, Float, and Fly* (Volume 15) contains three stories about Mickey, Donald, and Goofy. In *Animals and Their Babies* (Volume 5), Mowgli hears fascinating true stories about mammals from his jungle friends.